Project Jam Jar

– DARREN STANTON –

GW00673213

An environmentally friendly book printed and bound in England by
www.printondemand-worldwide.com

www.fast-print.net/store.php

PROJECT JAM JAR
Copyright © Darren Stanton 2011

ISBN 978-184426-975-4

First published 2011 by
FASTPRINT PUBLISHING
Peterborough, England.

Project: Jam Jar

This book is dedicated to the memory of my dad, Michael Stanton, who I sadly lost very suddenly and without warning in 2009. I always told my dad that one day I would write books and this is the first.

Everything I am and everything I will be is as a result of his lifelong support of every scheme, business, project and general crazy idea I ever had. Although he was a realist he never dismissed any of the ideas I had.

He had instilled in me from a very early age that anything is possible if you work hard and want it enough.

Many of the projects I attempted at an early age fell short of where I wanted them to be, but he always taught me to take it on the chin, learn from it and believe in myself and do better next time. Words can never express the absolute chasm that is left in my life without his support and knowledge.

As with every life performance or piece of work I ever do, I always dedicate it to my dad.

I also want to dedicate this book to my mum, Trisha, who has also told me I can achieve anything and be anyone I want to be but, above all: *"Just do what makes you happy"*

I also want to thank my partner, Sharon Simons, who has always supported me through thick and thin in every conceivable way. I have had some pretty crazy ideas over the years and she has never told me I was crazy, well once or twice she may have done but always supported me just the same.

The book is dedicated to the two most important people in the world to me, Trisha, my mum, and my partner Sharon who is an entrepreneur in her own right.

Acknowledgments

I want to take this opportunity to thank a few people who help and support me in the work that I do.

My good friends Ian Timothy and Liz from *Lizian* for their help and support they have shown me over many years of friendship.

My very talented friend, innovator, animator Mr Jason James (ghostboy.com) for his illustrations in this book and general unwavering support over many years.

A big thanks to Steve McComish and the rest of the team at *The London PR Company* for all their help and assistance in playing a significant part in my media success so far. I look forward to many more years of collaboration and success with Steve and the team.

To magician and underground mentalist Dee Christopher (www.deechristopher.com) for his help and support at all hours of the day and night. For those of you that know me, you will know that I have no concept of time and have no compunction in ringing people I need at any given hour of the day or night. Thankfully, the people I call, have accepted this is a quirky part of who I am.

I would like to thank *Waterstones* bookshop and all the staff at *Costa Coffee* in *Waterstones*, Nottingham. Especially my friend Louis Denny, who has kept me supplied with copious amounts of coffee during the 10 months I have camped out in the corner of their coffee shop. This book has been written whilst sat drinking coffee and performing impromptu mind games and various other mental jiggery-pokery, much to the delight of the customers. It is fair to say that I became very much a permanent fixture in the coffee shop. Not the most orthodox approach to writing a book I know, however, I have never been one for convention.

Preface

This book is also dedicated to those who dare to dream. To you I say, stay with it and persevere, never let anyone ever tell you cannot reach for the stars. History is littered with those who on paper should never have achieved anything but went on to achieve unimaginable success. As I shall show you, many of the world's most historic figures were told they would never achieve anything and went on to skyrocket in their field.

I also want you to consider that the graveyards are full of people who died with their best story still in them, never believing in themselves enough or to create the opportunities to tell their story or achieve their dream.

Apart from my family and a few others, I have had my share of negative people who told me I would never do it. You too may be surrounded by negative friends or family, or perhaps the people around you support you in every way.

When people are negative towards you when you voice your intentions, when you tell them all about your hopes and dreams and they scoff and tell you, "That will never work!", the language people use speaks volumes about them; it tells you what kind of person they are.

Listen not only to the way in which others respond to you but also how you, yourself communicate with yourself about things in your life.

I believe such negativity from others is fuelled by their own lack of confidence and frustration in their own situation and lack of success to achieve what they want in life. It is a kind of denial that better things exist out there. It is easier for those kinds of people to say to themselves,

"I could do it if I wanted to." They want to stay within their own comfort zone.

They are the same kinds of people who centuries before once thought the Earth was flat, that television would never replace radio as the main medium and that we would never put a man on the Moon.

In my experience, history repeats itself. The people may change but the attitudes sadly do not.

There is also an expression that says: **Birds of a feather flock together,** *and* in my opinion and experience, this is generally true. In any situation, especially in the workplace, likeminded people will always attract each other. Be it positive or negative.

I have trained many sales people in the course of my work, for example, and you will always find the less well-performing salespeople huddled together with their various excuses on why their sales figures are low. I have heard some weird and wonderful ideas over the years but the common denominator is never being themselves responsible for their results. It's always poor sales leads or the time of the year or if someone else is doing well then they must be having preferential treatment by the boss.

You may have experienced this or even be one of the negative people I have spoken about. You may be or may know someone who regularly uses language like:

"This is a nice idea but this hocus-pocus psycho stuff doesn't work on me, I'm too strong minded."

Or

"I've had that many knock-backs I just don't believe I'll ever get anywhere; maybe it's not to be."

Or

"I've done it all before, it doesn't work."

Sound familiar?

In speaking about people who are critical or unsupportive of your decision to improve or change things in your life, I am reminded of a quote by physicist Albert Einstein, who said:

"Great spirits have always encountered violent opposition from mediocre minds".

People who want to be different or to stand out from the crowd have always attracted or encountered ridicule or criticism from others. If you are receiving lots of criticism because you are not being supported in what you want to do, it's okay, you are in great company.

Maybe you have people around you who don't support you or maybe you do. Either way remember, this is down to you. Make your decision.

The thing to remember is that you cannot *directly* affect anyone else to support you or get them to change. However, as others begin to see change within you, you will notice they will change *indirectly* towards you as a consequence.

Now is the best time to have ever been alive to create the life you have always dreamt of. Opportunities and the ability to communicate with the whole world exist everywhere; you just need to find them.

Although we have never met, I believe in you.

Keep the faith and go for it!

Darren Stanton, Nottingham UK, December 2010

Chapter 1

I have been coaching, training and treating people clinically with this material for many years. As a result I have seen people, myself included, with the most negative of outlooks go on to achieve some miraculous results.

One of my most favourite methods of creating change is through the use of storytelling.

If you think back now to your childhood, maybe you have read stories or parables in the Bible, or whatever religious book applies to your faith. The commonality is that many of the core values and principles of any religion are taught in an indirect way through the use of stories and parables that have a deeper meaning and can be applied to your life. I have always loved stories that not only tell a story but also and have a much deeper meaning so that, just like the skin of an onion, we learn something new with every layer we penetrate.

I believe it makes more sense to people on a deep level. We all make the connection a lot quicker rather than if I give you immense amounts of psychological mumbo-jumbo.

Much of my style comes from Milton Erickson who was a doctor and fantastic hypnotherapist practising in the USA in the 1960s.

Although paralysed from polio and confined to a wheelchair, his style of therapy saw many clients making massive changes through his own unique style of hypnosis. The changes occurred in the client by their being told stories and metaphors. And most were not even aware that their therapy session had actually started when in fact it was nearly over. This was because Erickson used ***indirect*** methods of change as it is possible to create change conversationally.

Therefore this style became known as Ericksonian hypnosis of which I am a certified practitioner.

Perhaps like you, before I qualified in hypnosis or other change techniques, I equated it to being a Jedi knight from *Star Wars* I thought that somehow these new found skills would enable me to manipulate and affect others rapidly and even make others do things, even against their will. I learnt very quickly that this was far from the case and this was just a perception I had acquired from the media over the years.

I use the term hypnosis very loosely because my skills and abilities stem from many disciplines. The reality for me is that we are all hypnotists whether we believe it or not, or whether we are aware of it or not.

As we shall see later, the things that influence our behaviour and actions are by and large the same techniques someone qualified in change techniques employs to bring about a change in our behaviour.

You already have every skill you need within you to achieve whatever you want.

Do you drive?

Have you ever driven to the supermarket or to work and been thinking about something whilst still driving?

Have you ever got halfway to your destination without even realising it and wondered how you got there so quickly?

That's because the unconscious part of your mind has done the task hundreds of times before and engages in to a kind of autopilot.

Have you ever put your wallet or keys down and when you return they are gone?

You look high and low for them only to return to the place where you first looked and they were there all the time?

Yes, me to!

These are all common experiences we all share that demonstrate how the unconscious or autopilot part of our mind affects and directs us in our daily lives.

The truth is that the hypnotist has little or no power over us; it is the belief in his or her abilities that provides the power.

In a short while, I'm going to tell you a simple story which illustrates what the core value of my work is all about and serves as the premise for this book. Although I have heard many variations of the concept over the years, I like this version the best as it illustrates perfectly how we all follow a pattern of behaviour, some lasting our whole life.

You, like me, may well have done some sort of personal change programme in the past or bought some tapes or books only to give up a short time later.

You may be one of the people who has spent thousands of your hard-earned cash to go on supposedly life changing seminars only to find yourself still searching for your niche in life.

You know what happens; everyone begins with the best of intentions. New Year's resolutions are a fantastic example of a time in the year when people tend to make the decision to change. December is the month of overindulgence. We have all spent money like it's going out of fashion and we eat and drink like there's no tomorrow.

Research has shown that gym membership skyrockets in January and by the end of February a significant number of people have already forgotten about their decision to change. Christmas now seems a very distant memory and the daily grind of their old patterns and behaviours kick in. They begin to take action towards a goal and when results aren't showing straight away they give up and revert back to the old ways.

I have engaged in public speaking, writing newspaper articles, and appearing in the media and at seminars for many years. If you have ever attended one of my events you will have heard me tell the following story. For me, this story illustrates exactly what it feels like when we are in a place in our mind when, no matter what action we take, we do not get the result we wanted and we wonder why no matter what we do nothing seems to work.

The story goes something like this:

Imagine now you hold in your hand an empty old jam jar with a lid on it. Now imagine that we have placed a number of insects, let's say fleas, in the jar. You secure the lid to prevent their escape.

You sit there observing the behaviour of the fleas as they go about their business and you notice as they perform their natural function of jumping, the majority of the fleas begin hitting the lid, which obviously is quite painful. You then notice that after jumping many times although some of the fleas continue to hit the lid, the rest appear not to jump so high. This is because they have learnt that jumping with that level of force produces pain and therefore they adapt their behaviour to avoid the painful experience. They have evidence to support their newly acquired belief that taking that action hurts them.

When the fleas reach this point in the process, it is possible to remove the lid and notice that, remarkably, the fleas that stopped jumping so high remain firmly in the confines of the jar even though there is no longer any physical barrier preventing them from escaping. While the odd one jumps out to achieve freedom, the majority remain in the jar as if confined by some invisible force.

The reality is that those fleas that remain in the jar will probably spend the rest of their lives jumping up and down in that jar, never really exerting their full jumping potential, settling instead for mediocrity. They begin to behave in a way that is consistent with their previous experience of pain.

The bare reality is that unless they change their behaviour, they will probably die in that jar.

The question I want you to ask yourself is:

"Am I one of the fleas that have jumped out of the jar or are there areas in my life where I feel stuck in an impossible situation just like the fleas in that jar, thinking and feeling that no matter what I seem do, I never seem to get any good luck or success and the more action I seem to take the more stuck I seem to be?"

Project Jam Jar has therefore become the symbol for my passion and commitment for my message to reach as many people as possible through my book, forthcoming television series and live shows and seminars that you can achieve anything you desire.

I want you to at least consider that, on a level you are not yet even aware of, you already possess everything you need to achieve greatness and jump up and over any psychological barriers that until now may have kept you in your jam jar.

You really can do, have and be anything you want, if you are willing to do what's required.

Are you?

As you begin to think about where you are right now in your life, consider:

Is there a lid on your jar that until now you were not even aware of?

As you begin to think about previous life events where you didn't get what you want, like the fleas in the jam jar, did you change your response or did you just carry on doing what you always did or did you just give up and do something else? As you begin to think about it now, how much could these experiences be influencing how you see things now?

Do you want to jump out of your jar and achieve your dreams or do you want to stay as you are now, probably for the rest of your life, hitting the lid.

Do you want next year to be the same as this year?

If yes, then fine put down my book. Or do you want something to change in your life and to be in a different place next year?

Do you want the next five years to be the same as the last five?

The first step to creating change is discovering where you arc at the moment. If you were driving in your car trying to navigate yourself to an unfamiliar location, you first need to know where you are on the map before you can plan your route. A simple way of doing this is to begin to break aspects of your life down in to smaller chunks.

Below is a powerful task simply called:

The balance wheel

Each segment of the wheel represents a part of your life. If we imagine the centre of the wheel presents 0 and with you will see the numbers increase as they move out towards the number 5 on the outer wheel. Number 0 on the scale represents where you are currently not experiencing success. Number 5 means that you are totally happy in that area of your life.

Remember, this wheel is applicable only at the time of the exercise so as your experience changes so will the wheel.

I want you to begin on one of the segments and really think about where you would grade that aspect of your life using the 0-5 scale. Remember, there is no right or wrong. Be honest with yourself. Move through each segment and give each aspect of your life a rating.

The Balance Wheel

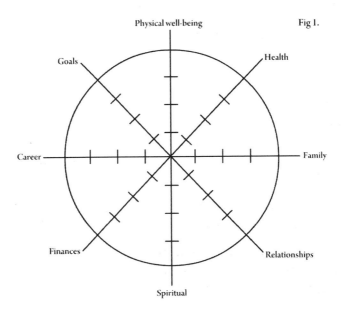

Fig 1.

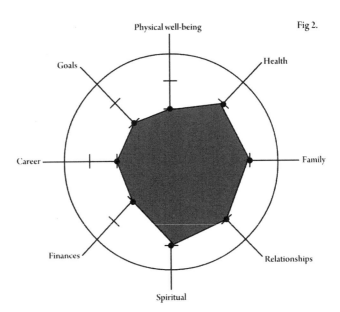

Fig 2.

When you have done that, I want you to join up the various dots all around the wheel; you will end up with some form of circular shape. Some of your segments may be on a 5 while others may be on a 0 or 1.

Good!

Now I want you to shade in the areas inside of your wheel (as illustrated in fig 2).

If you imagine this wheel was on your car or cycle, would it be a smooth ride or would it be a bumpy experience?

As you look at the areas that are the segments and the areas that have not been shaded in, can you see any similarity or connection between your results in the balance wheel and where you are currently experiencing difficulty or want change?

Maybe the results are a surprise or maybe they aren't, either way it will help you fine-tune your goal or outcome as we shall see later.

This exercise is not just for major life changes, you can use it for occurrences in life. I can often be seen scribbling on the back of some scrap of paper doing my balance wheel to help me see things more clearly.

Chapter 2

One powerful quote that I personally love, and have told myself thousands of times, comes from George Bernard Shaw but I have adopted it as my personal mantra:

"Some men see things as they are and say why? I dream things that never were and say why not!"

Firstly, thank you so much for buying this book.

Within these pages are the condensed theories, ideas and thoughts it has taken me over a decade to acquire.

When I teach an audience of people, I always begin with this understanding. I am going to present you with a new set of ideas about how you can finally begin to achieve the things you want in your life.

All I ask of you is this:

I am not asking you to accept everything I say as the truth. I do not profess that this book is a magic wand with the ability to grant you 3 wishes. The book assumes and begins from the point of view that you already understand that the buck stops with you. That you have reached a point in your life where you absolutely, positively have to change.

You are responsible from this point on for your life. Although destructive people or circumstances may have influenced you, or you perceive that others may have created the situation, you must accept from this point on total personal responsibility otherwise you will remain in your jar.

"You will never discover new oceans without first losing sight of the shore!"

For me, this means that we all need to trust ourselves and have the faith and belief to let go of what we know and feel comfortable with and to step outside of our comfort zone before we can truly change.

This is why people sometimes stay in a destructive relationship or a job or situation that doesn't serve them. People adopt an **"it's better the devil you know"** type mentality which perpetuates unhappiness.

Even though people know that their current situation is creating them unhappiness, they still continue to sit in their jar.

This material is very much like eating a buffet meal. You may love the chicken drumsticks but if you are vegetarian you may avoid them completely and opt for the cheese roll.

I would suggest using my book in the same manner. You can choose to trust in what I am saying totally and embrace all of my ideas or If some of what I tell you doesn't sit well, or you can't see or grasp how that would work for you, fine. Just go with the flow and see where it takes you. You can always go back to where you started if you don't feel empowered.

What I do know without any equivocation is that if you follow the tips, exercises and strategies, you will notice changes and others will notice the changes in you; it's as simple as that.

As my dad used to regularly remind me, the saying, **"You'll get out what you put in"**, is as true today with this material as it ever was.

There is a correlation between the effort and action you take and the results you obtain.

Remember, you are reading this material now for a reason. You already know on some level, now is the time to get what you want.

Now is your time.

As Gandhi once said:

"Be the change you want to see in your world".

As you move through the book, I would invite you take part in the exercises and tasks as that will give you the best possible chance of success.

I also want to thank you for making the decision to make changes in your life. You are very special because buying this book means that you fall within a very small percentage of the population who are prepared to take action and stick with it. How many of your friends do you know who have proclaimed they are making changes in their life only to give up a short time later?

Maybe you haven't bought it yet and are stood in the bookshop considering buying it or have downloaded it and are reading it on your device. You and I already both know, there is a reason you have been drawn to the book at this time in your life.

For me, there is no such thing as coincidence; I am a big believer in the concept of synchronicity. The concept that situations and people present themselves in to our lives at the appropriate time in order to allow us to progress. Just like you are already beginning to know that there is something within you that you are yet to achieve. Perhaps you already know what it is you want to change, or maybe you don't but do know you are not content.

Perhaps you have always been the odd one out, the one that always thought differently to the rest.

Maybe you feel you don't have the confidence to do it or maybe you do and you have negative and destructive people around you.

Chapter 3

After presenting some of my ideas to a group of people, one man once said, *"You're a freak and a madman, this stuff will never work for me."* The comment was not said in jest, it was said with some malice.

I thought about the comment and the man who had said it. The behaviour spoke much more about the pathology of the individual than about me. I simply replied with another quote of mine:

"There is a pleasure in being mad which none but madmen know."
John Dryden

For me, this means that until you have experienced something and have an intimate understanding of it firsthand, how can you offer an opinion or ridicule it?

When would NOW be the best time to make your decision to be the person you have always yearned to be?

My aim in writing this book is for you to learn a brand new set of skills and give you the opportunity to see things from a different point of view. You do not need to spend thousands of pounds on therapy or some other methods to discover why you have certain issues or feel that you are not where you imagined yourself to be at this point in your life.

You are not broken, you are unique.

Wherever you are in the world right now, you could potentially be standing on an area containing a rare and valuable commodity such as gold, oil or diamonds. You don't know though until you start excavating the ground and analysing the land around you and begin searching for what you want. You are exactly the same. Until you begin to search for the hidden qualities that already exist within you, you will never find them and your situation will continue.

This is your time, it doesn't matter what you've done in the past that hasn't worked for you.

I don't how many times you perceived yourself to have failed before. I don't care what has happened in the past, all I know is you can do whatever you want from this moment on.

The past does not equal the future. It is what you do now that counts.

As the American development coach Anthony Robbins says:

"It is in your moments of decision that your destiny is shaped".

Believe me, you are no different, you already possess rare and valuable commodities within you.

I am going to introduce you to some of the simplest but most empowering ways in which you can take action right now and quite literally begin to change your life and see massive results immediately.

There is an anecdote that says:

If you always do what you always did, then you will always get what you always got.

If you want something different then you have to do something different.

Chapter 4

It is thought that on average, as humans, we have at least 60,000 separate thoughts every day. These thoughts and patterns are the same ones we had last week, last month, last year. In fact, you may have been running these patterns for the last 20 years. I have worked with clients who have had specific issues for 30 years and then went on to achieve their goals.

I will be referring to the word *Pattern* in the course of the book. A Pattern relates to the idea that we know what works for us and because we are creatures of habit we stick to what we know because the result is pretty consistent and requires very little brainpower.

The mind is lazy and will find the path of least effort. An example of this might be where, if you drive a car, you may have had the experience of getting to a familiar destination without realising it, like driving home from work. You were still concentrating on driving and were perfectly safe. However because you have driven this route hundreds if not thousands of times, that part of your mind does it without thinking.

Can you relate to this example?

The vast majority of these 60,000 thoughts I mentioned never make it to the conscious level. The brain would probably blow a fuse and short-circuit if it had to consciously process every single thought.

Therefore the brain has certain processes to prevent it being overloaded.

When I am teaching a group of people my material, I often ask someone in the audience if they have some random skill like playing the violin or skydiving. Very often the question will be met with a blank, vacant expression and the reply, "Well, erm no."

I then ask, "How do you know?" Reply, "I've never tried."

Have you ever attempted a new skill such as golf or other sport, or some other task which under normal circumstances would require many years of practice to achieve competency, and you appeared to be relatively good straight away on the first attempt?

Some call it beginner's luck.

You see, when we think about doing something different or introducing something new into our lives, there is a simple four-part process of learning. It is a process we have all done and continue to do thousands and thousands of times.

Step 1

Unconscious incompetence

An idea you have never considered before. You are unaware of your ability to do the skill or not because you have never tried.

Step 2

Conscious incompetence

You try something new like playing a musical instrument or driving a car. By taking some action you gain feedback; you become aware of the fact that you do not yet possess the capability to do the skill and so gain some evidence from which you create the belief you cannot do something.

If the skill or ability is something of value to you, or is a skill which you need to acquire, then you will continue to improve. Practice makes perfect.

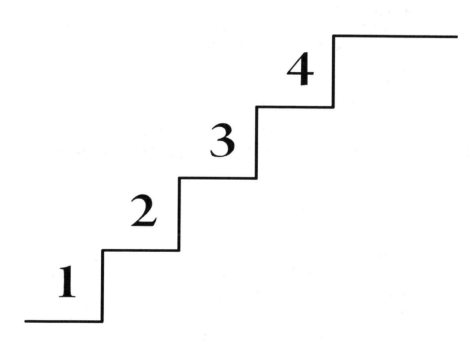

Step 3

Conscious Competence

A good example would be learning to drive. If you concentrate on the art of driving the car you can make gear changes, negotiate manoeuvres and parallel park whilst consciously concentrating. However, if your attention is distracted, such as the radio being on or someone talking to you, it breaks the spell and you lose the ability.

I remember when I was learning to play the piano, the countless hours of practising scales and various practice pieces. But it was an amazing feeling when after many hours practice things seemed to click as the capability moved from conscious incompetence (not having yet acquired the skill) to conscious competence (acquiring the skill) when the sounds coming out of the piano actually sounded amazing.

However, the minute I used to shout my dad to come and hear my amazing skill I would lose the skill as quickly as I acquired it because my attention was taken away from the piano to shouting my dad and by the time he had come to me, I lost the magic.

Perhaps you have childhood or other experiences, such as learning to ride a pedal cycle with the stabilisers or training wheels on to being able to ride unaided balancing on two wheels.

Step 4

Unconscious competence

This is the last stage of learning, which you, me and everyone else has attained infinite times. It is the autopilot stage of learning, where you can do things without the need for any conscious focus. Walking, talking, driving, playing an instrument, painting, speaking a foreign language, swimming without armbands etc.

You no doubt can think of countless more skills and abilities you have already acquired.

If you are learning new skills at the moment, notice what level you are at. People often get frustrated when results aren't showing. Know that if you are aware of where you are in the process, you already know now that if you continue to practise, you will move in to the unconscious competence stage very soon.

"Success is not a matter of chance; it is a matter of habit"

Successful people have habituated ways of being; it is not a onetime only event. They don't just use these techniques now and then. Just like you unconsciously use your destructive patterns at the moment, successful people are only running the same pattern as you except in a different direction. They have found a strategy that affects success and by repeating the process it has been hardwired in to the brain. They have learnt what they need to do in order to achieve success.

You see, success has a blueprint, a recipe, a pattern and a sequence.

As you continue to read, the blueprint will take shape as you are introduced to each part in turn.

I'm curious; as a child, did you ever help your parents bake food or perhaps you bake food with your children now? You probably began by getting all the ingredients together. The chances are you worked from a cookery book with all the recipes in there showing cooking times, quantities and what to do in order to produce the required result.

A cookbook contains recipe dishes which are tried and tested, if you follow the instruction to the letter, you are pretty much guaranteed to get the result you want. If you tried to make the food having never made it before and not following the instructions, you would most definitely get some result for your efforts but probably not as good as you wanted or expected. But if you liked cookery and continued learning, in time you, like a chef, could probably throw away the cookery book because you have baked dishes thousands of times and know how to do it without following the recipe.

Successful people are either consciously or unconsciously following the same process. If they are successful in one area of their life, they are generally successful in others because they apply the same strategy.

When we are born we are not supplied with an instruction manual, we just do the best we can with the apparent abilities we have. We inherit the rules of the game (i.e. life) from our parents or carers and life experiences.

I want you to think of this book as a sort of cookery book or instruction manual, with the only difference being you are not baking bread, you are following tried and tested instructions to achieve whatever it is you want.

Our blueprint of success consists of 4 distinct parts.

Many of us have dreams but how many of us really take action to achieve them?

There is an expression or concept I want to introduce you to which we will discuss in greater detail later:

"There is no such thing as failure, only feedback."

In the past when we have tried things that haven't succeeded or gone the way we had hoped, we probably perceived the result as a failure.

What I want you to do is begin to follow in the footsteps of the greats in history. I want you to treat every action you do towards what you want, not as a failure but as a result.

On the occasion of working towards the invention of the electric light bulb, a young journalist said to Thomas Edison:

"Mr Edison, how does it feel to have had over 10,000 failures at creating the electric light bulb?"

Edison replied:

"Young man, I have not had 10,000 failures, I have simply just discovered 10,000 ways that have not yet been successful."

When we think about famous people in life or history, we only remember them for their successes. We don't seem to contemplate that they had potentially thousands upon thousands of failures.

Goals are dreams with a deadline

When I studied the greats in history and looked at some of their quotes, I discovered that these quotes gave a clear insight into their mindset; into what they were thinking about in relation to what they were trying to achieve.

I have studied many of the world's top achievers and the one commonality I have discovered in all cases is that all of them had a very specific clear understanding of where they were going. They were not concerned with the how, they did not know *how* they were going to do it, they just knew that they would achieve their goal. I discovered that they all followed the same simple and distinctive process.

The first rocket to the Moon was the Ranger 4 rocket, which reached the Moon back in 1962.

If I told you that its intention was to reach the Moon, which it did, how accurately on course do you think this rocket was for the duration of its journey?

100% 75%, 30%?

Have a guess, the answer appears later.

If I was to offer you a simple four-part process to achieve anything you want in life, I'm curious, would you take it?

The truth is, you have done this process and continue to do this process every day, but don't even realise it.

If you completed the balance wheel exercise, you may have discovered an area of your life in which you want to improve or change.

I want you to choose a goal, or what I shall from now on call an *outcome*, to work towards.

From every action you take you will get a result or outcome. We shall not from this point on concern ourselves with whether it was a success or failure but rather with what we can learn from the outcome you get.

Remember the quote I gave you earlier?

There is no such thing as failure only feedback.

Every 'outcome or result' is an opportunity to discover something new.

The first step in our success is to set our outcome. What is it you want? If it's a car, what make of car?

What specification?

What colour? You need to be specific.

How many doors?

Imagine sitting in it now. How does it feel?

What's the stereo sound like?

Is it petrol or diesel?

Many people do not achieve their goals because they have not been specific enough with their outcome. Unless you have a very clearly defined outcome, how will you or your unconscious mind ever know that you have achieved it?

If it's confidence, how will you feel when you are confident?

What will it be like?

What will let others know that you have changed? What will they see and hear in you that will be different?

If you do not have any conscious expectation of what confidence is, how will you know when it has arrived?

If confidence was a colour, what colour would it be?

Begin to build up your goals into a 3-dimension experience in your mind. Be very specific in what you will experience when you have achieved your goal.

Chapter 5

A few years ago I used to teach on a programme preparing new entrepreneurs in writing a business plan moving towards the launch of their business idea. My input was making them aware of the psychology of running a business, motivation and belief techniques and so on.

It was clear from the outset that many of the people I met had some pretty unrealistic expectations when it came to how quickly they would rise to business superstardom. Many of the students thought they would be the one who would be a millionaire in 30 days with their idea.

I was teaching the group of about 30 people and the material being discussed was about the importance of setting goals and realistic achievable outcomes. I suggested setting small achievable goals. For example, that the first paying customer you get through the door means that you are now successful and in business, rather than having a mindset that you are not successful until you can go out and buy a Mercedes car for cash.

It has been discovered that many successful people keep a journal about their experiences and successes; I suggested it would be good to do a nightly review. That is to simply ask yourself three questions each evening and jot down your honest responses.

There is great benefit to sitting down at the end of the week and seeing all of the crossings out in your journal, your week's successes; and even more motivational at the end of the month.

This is a tried and tested action and I invite you to do the same as you begin your journey of change and discovery.

There are only 3 simple questions I want you to ask yourself at the end of every day.

What went well today?

Write down everything that you felt you achieved no matter how small or insignificant you feel it is.

What didn't go to plan today?

You will note from the way I have phrased the question, it is not asking what failed or what was a disaster, it is asking what happened that you hadn't anticipated or planned to happen.

How did you respond? What was your result or outcome?

What did I learn from today and what will I do differently tomorrow?

If the same thing happened tomorrow, would you respond in the same way if you were happy with the result or would you do something differently next time?

One of the more robust students said that he would only feel successful when he had £1million in the bank. I said that by stating that success would only mean having that money was unproductive as he would have achieved success long before that and that he would probably lose motivation long before becoming a millionaire. This individual dismissed this notion and retained his idea that success meant being a millionaire.

Following the completion of the course, I began to hear good things about this person in terms of his being very successful. And later that year, I saw him in a coffee shop and we had a chat about his successes.

He had started with nothing and in 2 years he was turning over £60,000 and employed 3 people. From his posture and the way he spoke, I could see that as he told me about his business there was a clear contradiction in his body language and how he was conducting himself.

He said that he considered himself to be a failure despite all of his friends and family being very proud of his achievements. He felt a failure despite all of this because he had continually told himself that success meant having £1million in the bank.

Although his life had changed immensely, with a better car, the ability to move house and have more cash at his disposal, he was still very unhappy. Even though all of the signs of success were present, he could not see what everyone else was seeing.

My point is that I believe this person had all the focus, determination and passion to go on to be a millionaire. However, I understood where his frustration came from.

I coached this person for a few months and he understood the importance of re-evaluating his goals and outcomes. He realised that he had surpassed many of the pitfalls many of his classmates had already given up on and ceased trading.

I have no doubt that his person will indeed go on to be a millionaire. The reality is that he will probably far exceed that figure and not even notice since his focus on what is important has now changed.

The point of the story is that it's okay to have a goal of becoming a millionaire. However, if he had created lots of small outcomes from the outset, he would have had the feeling of success many times that would have given him the value in his life he wanted. When you have a specific idea of what you want, you move on to the next stage.

First, a little story originating from the Buddhist philosophy.

The monk and the thief

Many hundreds of years ago in a remote part of the world, there was a young boy who was an orphan with no one but himself in the world.

Life had shaped him in to what he was and he had survived and had endured many hardships.

The boy had survived on the streets by using his wits and cunning and had developed in to a very proficient thief and pickpocket. The skills he had acquired meant literally the difference between life and death.

One day, he came across a new town he had never seen before; high on the hill he spied a monastery.

He thought, 'hmmm, the churches are very rich indeed, there will be riches beyond my wildest dream up there and lots of good food'.

In anticipation, he climbed up the steep hill until he finally reached the monastery and pressed his little hands and nose up against the cold stained glass window to look inside for 'opportunities'. He observed an old lonely monk sitting in front of a roaring fire, polishing golden candlesticks and other expensive looking relics.

'If I got hold of just one of those candlesticks, I could eat like a king for a year', the thief thought to himself.

As the thief continued to watch him, the monk needed clean rags for the rest of the polishing and needed to enter the other room to get them. As the monk walked towards the doorway, he suddenly walked towards a solid stone wall and walked straight through it as if he were a ghost, returning a short time later with the rags and continuing polishing.

The thief looked on in astonishment, he could hardly believe what he had seen. He thought to himself that if he could acquire that ability, why there would be no fortress or building that would prevent him from entering. He could be rich beyond imagination.

With this in mind, he went to the heavy wooden door and began to knock. The monk eventually answered the door and the thief begged the monk for food, shelter and a bed for the night. The monk agreed and let him in.

Days later, after many hearty meals, the thief used his influence and persuasion on the monk, so much so that he convinced the monk to take him on as his pupil. All the time with the ulterior motive that during the course of his studies he would surely be taught how to walk through walls.

Many weeks and months passed and the thief grew impatient of waiting until finally he said to the monk:

"When I first came here, I oversaw you walk through the wall, when will I be taught that?"

The monk reassured the thief that all good things come to those who wait and with that, although a little frustrated, the thief continued to study the holy book and to do his chores diligently and without question.

Three years of hard work and study passed, until one day the thief again grew impatient and asked the monk:

"Father, when will you teach me to walk through the wall?"

The monk replied:

"My son, you are doing well and are a fine student, continue with what you are doing and in time you will learn all that you desire."

This reply didn't really please the thief and made him even more angry and frustrated; however, he thought to himself that all the time and effort he had already invested would be rewarded if he could leave the monastery with the power to walk through walls and so returned to his duties.

Two more long years passed until the thief became resolute in his decision to now be taught that which he had laboured for. He again pleaded with the monk finally to teach him to walk through walls. The monk replied:

"My young friend, you have studied well and worked hard and I think the time has now come for you to learn how to walk through walls. Go now in to the next room and fetch me the clean cloths so that we may begin your first lesson."

With happiness and excitement at the thought of finally gaining this power, the thief quickly hurried towards the door. But instead of using the door as usual, he approached the wall and in his moment of passion and excitement walked straight through the solid stone wall, as if he were a ghost. A short time later he diligently returned with the cloths in hand, sitting down in front of the monk for his lesson but never even realising what he had just done.

What can we learn from this story?

For me, the thief acquired the skill of walking through the wall much earlier than he ever realised.

Maybe, like the thief you are asking for something you already have or at least you already possess the skill or personal quality you desire on some level you are not aware of?

Like many skills we acquire, we cannot pinpoint the exact moment we learnt the skill and were able to do it unconsciously without thinking.

What qualities, skills and abilities do you have hidden deep within you that you are not even aware of?

Can you recall the precise moment you learnt to swim without water wings or armbands?

The exact moment you could read?

The moment you could drive a car?

The exact moment you could tie your own shoelace?

The moment you could walk?

My guess is no.

Always keep in mind, although you want to make changes and achieve things in your life, like the thief, you may be much closer than you could ever know. Like the thief, during your journey towards what you want, you may get frustrated, angry and maybe even wonder if all the effort is worth it.

Just like the thief, your efforts will be rewarded and when you think your success is a long way off, you suddenly begin to make a breakthrough in what you are doing.

Remember, change will not suddenly flash in your face; you will not wake the next morning 30 pounds lighter or £10,000 richer. Success comes gradually and subtly. Just like you have learnt to do anything else in your life, your hopes and aspirations appear in the same way.

Is it all worth the effort? The answer is a resounding, YES!

I am sure in life, we have all seen individuals that talk a good game but never seem to put their money where their mouth is, so to speak. The sort of person who says they will conquer the world but never seems to do anything about it.

A brilliantly crafted specific outcome is pointless without the second part of the process which the:

Take action

It sounds so simple doesn't it. You would be amazed at the amount of clients I have worked with who quite literally have an abundance of skills and abilities but have not done anything about it.

When you take action towards a goal, one of two things will happen: you will get the result you expected or you won't. What makes the difference between success and failure is the meaning we give to the result or outcome.

Not getting the result you wanted does not mean that you failed, all it means, and all it has ever really meant, is that it is an outcome, nothing more.

The third part of the process is:

Respond to feedback.

Successful people do not treat an unexpected result as a failure, rather, they see the unexpected as an opportunity to learn from. They look at where the result places them in relation to where they are heading. They see every result from their actions as a means to gauge their next step.

The fourth and final part of the process is:

Flexibility.

You need to be flexible enough in order to respond to the feedback. Now, that does not mean bending over and touching your toes, it means that when things are not going in the direction you want and results aren't showing, you are flexible enough to realise you may need to change your approach.

Flexibility is the stage at which a lot of people give up because they get frustrated when results don't show. And they keep doing the same sort of action and, guess what, they get the same result which in turn creates even more frustration.

Being aware of how you respond to things is important because once you realise how you respond, you can decide how you would rather have things be.

Consciously deciding to change begins to affect important parts of your brain.

So to recap.

Set your goal or outcome - be specific. Take action.

Respond to feedback.

Be flexible.

Do you remember my question about the first rocket to the Moon and I asked you to think about how accurately on course it was?

The answer was actually 3%

Was that massively different to what you had or did you have something similar? If not, let me explain.

The rocket followed the same four-part process we have just looked at:

It set its **outcome** - getting to the Moon

It blasted off - **took action**

Once in the sky, the rocket used its instrumentations to determine where it was in relation to the Moon and because of gravitational pull and other forces, it responded to **feedback.**

It was then **flexible** enough to use its engines to put it back on track.

The rocket therefore was repeating this process until it reached the Moon. It travelled in a zigzag motion from left to right.

It has been suggested that when humans achieve what they want no matter how small, they have actually followed a similar pattern.

Think about when you learnt to walk or learnt to drive or learnt some other skill. It was the same process you went through.

Chapter 6

It's all in your head!

In our brains, there is a cluster of cells called the Reticular Activating System or RAS. It is the job of the RAS to filter out all the extraneous or unwanted information and the rest makes it in to the conscious mind for processing.

Another way of explaining this is to imagine a fishing net. The net will catch only fish large enough to get caught due to the size of the holes and the smaller fish will be able to escape and swim away.

I'm curious, have you ever been looking to buy a specific kind of car and the more you go about your day, the more you begin to notice that suddenly everyone has got that very same car?

Have you ever bought some new clothes and suddenly everyone seems to have copied you and you notice more and more people seem to be dressed the same as you?

Have you ever put your car keys down and when you return to pick them up they are gone, only for you to find them in the very same place later?

A friend I have is expecting a baby at the moment and she said a curious thing which highlighted the point to me. She said:

"It's *really funny, wherever I go at the moment everyone seems to be expecting a baby as well.*"

Do any of these experiences ring true or strike a chord with you?

This comment is really significant and gives an insight in to my friend's perception. From her comment, the implication is that there is an increase in the amount of the population having a baby. This is a fantastic way in which the RAS is affecting my friend's conscious awareness. It is only because the RAS is filtering for any data relating to pregnancy because it is personal to her at that specific moment.

These are common experiences we can probably all relate to as examples of how the mind discriminates over what you are allowed to be consciously aware of.

This book is the story of how you, me and everyone can have more choice, power and control over our lives and achieve whatever we want.

Knowledge is, after all, power so they say.

Warning:

With this book comes a serious caution. By continuing to read this book, **you will change**. You are giving yourself permission to change. When change occurs there is a consequence. For every action there is a reaction. Everything has to be in balance. As with the ecology of the rain forest, when parts of it are destroyed there is a global consequence.

There is also the theory that the movement of butterfly wings in one part of the world can have a consequence somewhere on the other side of the world.

The human mind is no different. Be aware, when you change, other things will have to change and adapt in order to remain congruent, in order to accommodate your new ways of thinking and being.

Did you ever see the movie from the 1980s *Back to the Future*?

In the movie, where the Michael J Fox character uses a time machine to go back to 1955, whenever he intervened in the past and returned to his own time there was a consequence back in 1985. The difference is that the changes you will be making, you will be in total control of.

It's like moving in to a new house, or moving to a new location. Things will seem unfamiliar and strange at first but you will soon become familiar with your new surroundings and behaviours.

The chances are that most of your friends will support your lifestyle changes and you will attract new friends and inevitably lose friends as they will no longer feel you are the same as you once were. Take this as a very positive reaction and sure sign you are becoming more like the person you want to be.

An example of the consequences of making changes was when I had a client who came to see me as a private clinical client. After trying 'everything' she could to improve her weight, she wanted to see if I could help her achieve her goal. All of her circle of friends had weight issues and it was the glue and commonality that held the circle together.

They used to attend a well known weight loss group together etc.

Following a number of sessions, this client, let's call her Jane, made very noticeable changes and after a short time improved her weight considerably. She began to go to the gym, something she previously would never have done, which accelerated her results.

Then Jane began to notice that her friends changed in regards to their attitudes to her. Some were supportive while the majority was not and she thought that she must have offended them in some way.

As Jane continued to improve her weight, this had a generative effect because as she lost weight, her confidence improved.

As her confidence improved, her other life goals changed with it.

This concerned Jane because she couldn't understand why some of her friends had stopped calling her as they once did. She continued to be friends with some of the circle whilst not with others as they could not accept her for the person she had become because her development had changed then others in an indirect way.

The point to the story is that I am stressing the importance of the ecology of making changes. Be prepared for not only the supportive people but others who will change sometimes for the not so good.

"The mind once stretched by new ideas never regains its original dimension." *Thoreau*

For me, success is not just about finding a cure for an illness or becoming a zillionaire. Not everyone wants to own a BMW. Success comes in many forms.

When I do seminars I have hundreds of people in the audience and

I ask the question:

"If I had the ability to grant you the wish of feeling wealthy, what would I need to give you right now?"

Depending on people's position and circumstance, many will interpret the question to be specifically about money. Some people say £1000, others may say £100,000.

However, others may interpret the question in terms of wealth relating to health, spiritual or relationships. I have had people say, "I just want to healthy, that would be wealth to me."

The point I'm making here is, whatever it is you want, no matter how big or small it is, I don't care. As long as you are prepared to take the action required to achieve it and follow the four-part outcome process and you believe it will happen, it will.

Have you ever seen those snow domes? The little plastic bubble filled with water, you generally see them at Christmas time with a snowman. You shake them and see all of the snow displace itself and slowly drift down creating a snowy scene.

The mind is very similar. When we begin to think differently, it is the same as giving the mind a good shake which in turn allows us to see things differently.

As the earlier saying said:

"The mind once stretched by new ideas never regains its original dimension".

What follows are some tasks designed to shake the mind in much the same way. Maybe these are exercises you have seen before in other training or psychology books. If you haven't, let's have a look at a few new ideas.

We all have our own way of approaching tasks or challenges. You are already probably aware that you are very good at certain tasks or skills and probably not so good at others. That is because you have a natural aptitude for certain things.

There is no right way or wrong way to approach these tasks.

Grab a piece of paper and a pen and have a go at the following mind games.

Look at the text below and as you look, I want you to count every time the letter **F** appears in the text.

Finished files are the result of years of scientific study combined with the experience of years.

Write down or remember your response. The answers and explanations appear later in the book.

Now I want you to look at the text in the two triangles on the next page. I want you to instinctively write down what you see.

Ready for the next one?

Now I am going to attempt to use my linguistic influence and persuasion skills and abilities in the mind game shown below. I want you to choose one of the cards on the next page in your mind, look at it and focus even more. Nothing else matters but focusing all of your attention on your chosen card.

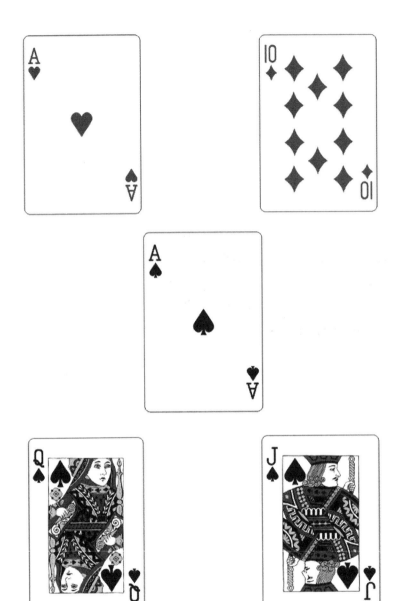

I want you to look at your watch or phone and say the current time of day to yourself.

before you turn over the page. If I have been successful in my outcome, you **WILL NOT** see your chosen card.

Now turn over and see.

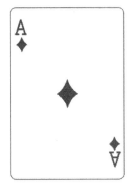

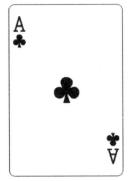

Do you see your chosen card or have I been successful in influencing your decision?

So how did you do with the little tasks? How many F's did you notice - 3? 4? or more? Well there were actually 6 letter F's in that passage. Did you get 6 or something else?

The explanation is below.

"*F*inished *f*iles are the result *of* years *of* scientific study combined with the experience *of* years.

Almost everyone guesses three. Why?

It seems that the brain cannot correctly process the word 'of'. The letter F usually makes the 'f' sound, like in 'fox'. However, in the word 'of', it makes a 'v' sound. Somehow, your brain overlooks the word 'of' as it scans for the sound of 'f'.

So if you didn't guess correctly, don't feel too badly about it. The test is designed to highlight how the brain can very often miss information even when it is right in front of you.

On the second mind game, did you read:

"**Paris in the springtime**" or something else?

"**A bird in the hand**" or something else?

If you still haven't spotted the deliberate error, it is that the word 'THE' is repeated but the mind generally just skim reads it. If you don't believe me skip back and double check.

The mind game with the playing cards was really nothing to do with influence and persuasion. Whichever card you chose on the first page would have been successful, since every card on the second page is different. Because I placed so much emphasis on zeroing in and focusing on one card alone, the mind does not consider that every card was different.

As you consider the results you got in the mind games, could the same psychological principle be at work in other areas of your life? Perhaps you have made decisions in the past based on the circumstances in front of you only to have regretted them later?

This idea is called '**The psychological blind spot**'.

There is a famous piece of research which demonstrates the concept of the psychological blind spot brilliantly. In the research, a group of people are asked to watch a piece of footage of a group passing a basketball to each other. Half of the 'on screen' participants have on black T-shirts and the other half white.

Half of the observers are tasked to observe how many times the people in white shirts pass the ball to each other and the other half the ones wearing black T-shirts.

At the end of the exercise the groups are asked for their results with the addition of, "Did you see the gorilla?"

The group is naturally very confused at being asked about seeing a gorilla. But halfway through the sequence there is someone dressed in a gorilla suit that stands in the centre of the screen and beats its chests before walking off.

In the study, very few of the group saw the gorilla. They were so focused and locked on to the task of observing basketball passes that they never saw the gorilla. This demonstrates how we can all fail to see things happening in front of us when the mind is intently focused on something else.

If you want to explore this concept in greater depth visit www.viscog.com

Professor Richard Wiseman, who is a psychologist and magician working at the University of Hertfordshire, wrote a fantastic book on the whole notion of psychological blind spots called, surprisingly, **Did you see the gorilla?** It is definitely worth a read.

All of the above are designed to demonstrate how we can miss information despite things being right in front of us, and how by being aware of how our mind works we can open up more opportunities for ourselves.

The above seeks to demonstrate the importance of looking at the big picture and of how, when the mind focuses on something like worries or concerns very intently, we can shut out all other possible solutions and opportunities available to us because of where our attention is flowing.

Chapter 7

I had always been very much a people person, sensitive to other people, and it was no great surprise I ended up doing the job I do.

As an entrepreneur, I have been involved in numerous different businesses and crazy, get rich schemes; some worked fantastically and some sunk faster than the *Titanic*.

Don't be disheartened if you still haven't found your niche in life yet. Some of the most interesting people I have ever met are still undecided what they want to do but they are enjoying their journey.

During my life, I am amazed that I have had so many jobs. At one time or another in my life I have worked as an actor, salesman, police officer, sales trainer, musician (I play the piano), market trader plus lots more. I believe all of the roles I was attracted to have one commonality; they were all concerned with people. I just realize now that I was searching for my place in the world.

For the past ten years I have made my living from stepping inside people's heads. From helping people overcoming phobias, showing people how to become powerfully confident through live performances, showing thousands how to run their brain.

If you believe the press, I am considered one of the UK's leading experts on body language and lie detection techniques. During the summer of 2010, I had the honour of being asked by the UK's media to consult as body language expert analysing the performance of the three party leaders. It was a fantastic opportunity and the experience taught me so much about the psychology and importance of having the ability to send out the right messages to your listener and just how powerful and influential the mass media actually is.

When all is said and done though, I only have two things going for me; I have always had a love of people and always been fiercely passionate about everything I have ever done.

There is a Chinese proverb that says:

"If you find that thing you love, if you devote your life and you're passion to it, then you will never have to work another day in your life".

This is something I have adhered to throughout my life. Simplistic I know but just imagine if you could create a lifestyle around you where your whole life was pretty much as you wanted it to be.

I have never been able to accept things as they are. Ever since I can remember, I have hated injustice and being a childhood victim of bullying, paradoxically, made me a great lover of people. Rather than assuming the role of a victim, I was fascinated by the bully, who we shall call, *John,* behaved as he did.

Although I failed every exam at school, I knew I was different, not better than the rest just different. It was no great surprise then that I ultimately later studied psychology together with an array of behavioural science disciplines all to do with personal development.

I read literally hundreds of books, attended all the seminars I could afford to go on. I studied psychology, neurolinguistic programming - the study of excellence developed by Dr John Grinder and Dr Richard Bandler. I also studied many other strands of clinical and stage hypnosis, and learnt the psychology of lies and deception training.

I became a proverbial 'sponge' for knowledge and understanding of the mind and continue to do this on a continued basis through continued professional development.

As a result of my study, I hold the right and privilege to call myself a 'Master' in my art and craft. However, I believe you can never really become a master of anything because this implies you have attained a level of all-knowing and cannot proceed any further. I would suggest that we never achieve a state where we cannot learn something new.

I began my career as a clinical hypnotherapist and psychological coach where I helped my clients overcome issues from fears, phobias, confidence and smoking, and pitched myself as a one-stop shop for change. I made a name for myself which made me stand out from the rest of my peers in that I made the bold claim that rather than spending weeks, months or years trying to solve your issue I would help you overcome it in one session.

My strap line or unique selling point became:

No change, no *charge* !

I became involved in a mind, body and spirit show or psychic fair circuit where I was suddenly on stage being billed as 'The Phobia Buster'. It was fantastic experience, both good and not so good. I was under pressure, which I loved, as I had no idea who or what issue would be wheeled out in front of me next.

I spent the few years travelling from place to place in my old Peugeot car putting on shows and demonstrations, breaking down on the motorway more than once. This experience gave me a great passion for performance and allowed me to get the same rapid results I was getting in the private treatment room but to a great many more people and, of course, it allowed me to make a better living.

The people I met and the experience I gained from those years have proved an invaluable grounding to this day.

Someone once said to me, "Darren, if you want to know what you're good at, look at what you are interested in."

They were right because I absolutely love what I do and I am extremely privileged that I can make my living from doing the thing that is clearly my passion.

I have known many people in my life who have had a fantastic idea for a business or some other idea and seem really motivated at the time but a few weeks later, when I ask how their idea is coming along, they have given up already.

You may know or have been the kind of person who employs the blame strategy or what I call the scarcity mentality. That is, blaming someone else or circumstances, something that is beyond your control as a means to justify your lack of success. It is often easier to blame someone else's apparent inaction as the catalyst or reason for your failures.

Successful people make things happen; they are proactive and not reactive and will not use other people as a means to justify their lack of results. They do not dwell on past events. They will learn from them but they do not allow past experience to affect what they want.

THERE IS NO ONE ELSE TO DO THIS, THERE'S ONLY YOU!

It is therefore very important, as we shall look at later, to set realistic, achievable goals which keep you motivated by seeing your achievements daily. The most successful people in life are the ones who write down their goals and make small measurable goals moving towards the overall bigger goal.

Successful people make a 'to do' list where they break down the tasks they need to achieve and continue to break things down in to small manageable chunks. I can very often be seen scribbling new ideas or writing a 'to do' list on the back of a napkin in the absence of my notepad.

If you can identify with feeling like you are stuck in a rut and success hasn't found you yet, that's because you have taught yourself unconsciously to take only the action which will produce the result you expect.

Now I know at first glance you may think, What! I don't like my job and I want to leave! So let me get this right Darren, you're telling me I'm keeping myself there?

Yes that's exactly what I'm saying.

It's a hard pill to swallow and with a few minor exceptions you are responsible for where you are in life.

Now I recognise that at this point the chances are that you probably disagree with me and put down the book. When I was told this many years ago, I had a very adverse reaction to the thought that someone was telling me it was all down to me, and it was my perceived failures were down to me. Don't let that potential feeling of disagreement be a negative thing. Know that that feeling of resistance comes from the conscious mind not the unconscious one and it is the unconscious mind that we are dealing with.

It's not what ultimately happens to us that shapes who we are it's how we see the situation. What is a catastrophe to one person is a small challenge to another.

When you accept this bitter pill that your current situation is a consequence of your past thoughts and actions and by also accepting that you are responsible for your future successes.

When you accept that no one is responsible for you but you, you will achieve freedom you have never known. To realise and know that you have the power, choice and control in your life is a fantastic feeling.

Your current reality, the job, the car, the partner, the money, the circumstance are all a physical manifestation of your beliefs about life.

As we shall see shortly, your beliefs about things control your responses in life and ultimately the life around you. Your life is a physical creation of the mental blueprint you currently hold in your mind.

The difference between people who appear to achieve whatever they want and those who don't is their ability to recognise how to make small changes and how to change things in their heads at certain times to get what they want.

The truth is that many of the ideas that I'm presenting are not new. They have been used for centuries by many of history's most significant individuals and continue to be used by some of the world's top achievers.

The beauty of these techniques is that you can begin right now. You can get results today just by beginning to make subtle changes in your life and the way you are thinking. It's simple, change your mind, change your world.

Chapter 8

When you were a child, did you believe in Father Christmas? Did you leave out your glass of wine and a mince pie for Santa Claus? If you were brought up in a western culture as a child then I'm guessing, like many other children, that you did in the expectancy that as you'd been a good little boy or girl all year you would find a nice surprise come Christmas morning.

Maybe you have children of your own now and if they are young enough they believe it too. They learnt the belief from you.

The question is why don't you believe in him now?

The truth is that you acquired the idea of Santa Claus from your parents as perhaps your children have from you. Can you remember the point at which your belief changed and you no longer believed in him? You gained new information you were not previously aware of, then your unconscious mind automatically shifted in order to align itself in order to remain congruent with the new belief. And the new belief was manifested in you no longer leaving out your wine and mince pie.

As you think back now, perhaps you can remember lots that you may have believed in before but no longer to do.

The concepts that I'm presenting to you are not new to you, it's something you have done an infinite number of times, just unknowingly. Just as in years to come as you look back to now your beliefs may have shifted about something you currently truly believe to be correct.

We as humans are not static, we are continually moving.

If you can remember back to the time that you believed in Santa Claus, you totally believed in the concept and in that moment truly believed that it was the fat man in a red suit eating the mince pie.

Life is much the same, much of what we believe comes from our upbringing, such as our parents or care givers and later on from our environment.

I was once travelling up the M1 Motorway (a *major road in the UK which connects the South of England to the North*) towards Leeds in Yorkshire for a business meeting together with a colleague. As we travelled along I noticed that a few times during the course of the journey he raised his index and second finger up to his head in a salute-style gesture. As a keen observer of human behaviour, I was intrigued by what I had seen and I just had to ask him what the saluting was all about.

He explained that he was just saluting the magpies (small black and white birds). He said, "Everyone salutes them, it's normal."

I explained that I had never seen it before and that I don't do it and that it was not that common. He said that he had seen his parents do it as a child and as far back as he remembered he had always done it.

I asked him what would happen if he didn't salute the bird and he replied, "Well, everyone knows you get bad luck if you don't salute them."

I said, "Have you ever not saluted them and still had good luck?"

He replied, "I don't know because I don't want to take the risk."

Later in the year I was invited to his house during the summer for a BBQ when his parents and children were there. As we sat in the garden a magpie flew past and sure enough the whole family suddenly saluted the magpie simultaneously. It was fascinating to see the power of beliefs truly in action.

Maybe this is something you do yourself or you may be aware of other habits or unusual things you have always done. Many of your day-to-day actions, believe me or not, have been unconsciously inherited from your parents or carers.

What is the force that determines whether we are successful in our lives or not? It's our beliefs about what is possible or not.

In the Haitian culture, for example, there is a big belief about the deadly power held by the witch doctor. People who have been cursed by the witch doctor have died as a result. But the real killer is not magic it is the certainty in the belief that the doctor really does have the power to kill you.

Now you may not have been cursed by a witch doctor but what other deadly beliefs do you currently hold that have stopped you from doing what you want in life? Beliefs have the power to create greatness and the power to destroy.

Superstitions are one such fascinating example. They are an inherited or learnt behaviour whereby you either avoid certain situations, such as walking on the cracks in the pavement, or you have to engage in some ritualistic behaviour such as saluting magpies. The general consequence of engaging in the behaviour is to avoid some kind of 'bad luck' or some other unpleasantness.

This list is by no means exhaustive but some commonly held superstitions include:

- Walking on cracks in the pavement - brings bad luck

- Swinging a door – summons the devil

- Putting shoes on a table, - brings bad luck

- Spilling salt - must throw over left shoulder to avoid bad luck

- Walking under a ladder - brings misfortune

- Crossing over on the stairs - bad luck

- Washing clothes on New Year's – washes someone out of the family, i.e. will induce a death in the family.

You may perhaps be able to think of many more. All the triggers produce a certain behaviour.

Superstitions are a good example of how a particular behaviour can become wired in to the brain and then last a lifetime without the person ever really knowing why. If you have a superstition, I would take a gamble at this point that one or both of your parents have the same superstition as well as your children.

People who subscribe to superstitions will almost always be able to produce the evidence to support their belief. Very often it is anecdotal evidence, i.e. it happened to a friend of a friend etc.

Fears and phobias are another classic example of how a piece of behaviour can be indirectly hardwired in to someone's unconscious mind.

During my initial assessment of clinical clients, I take a very thorough history which includes any topics of interest regarding parents or carers. A significantly high proportion of clients I have worked with for a phobic type reaction reported that their parents also had the same fear or phobia.

I am sure that other professional therapists would agree when I say that in my experience a very small percentage of phobic clients presented to them have a specific incident which they attribute to the onset of the phobic response.

Some common phobias are spiders, rats, heights, enclosed spaces, social situations, clowns, medicals and open spaces. And the most commonly held fear or phobia in the UK, believe it or not, is ....public speaking.

I work with more clients for public speaking that any other. It could be a presentation at work, giving a speech at a wedding, but whatever the occasion I have seen very successful professional people reduced to quivering wrecks at the mere thought of standing at the front speaking. I suppose it is because it is a very unnatural place to be.

I was once being interviewed on national radio about my work and as this show was the breakfast show it probably attracted listeners of around the many hundreds of thousands.

I asked the presenter if he was doing any TV work and to my surprise he told me that although he was a very successful radio presenter, if he thought about the listeners as real people he would start to get very nervous and feel unwell. He said that when he thought about the listeners in his head, he just used to see the image of thousands of big eyes looking at him.

He said that when he is on air he just imagines he is talking to some very good friends and that is how he learnt to resolve his issue.
Someone you would never have assumed to have an issue with public speaking.

The reality is that some of the things people consider themselves to have a phobia about are really nothing to do with it.

Let me elaborate.

When someone raises their hand towards you with a handshake gesture, do you raise yours in response? Of course you do because your mind has learnt to recognise their raised hand as a psychological cue for you to complete the cycle.

If you drive, do you stop at a red traffic light? If you don't, you suffer the consequences of either a traffic ticket or having a car accident.

You are programmed with thousands of similar learnt responses, some good some not so good.

Scientists have discovered that there are some communities in remote parts of the world where if you raised your hand to shake hands they will look at you in a confused manner and they would certainly not respond to a red traffic light.

We are a complex mixture of learnt behaviours consisting of triggers and responses.

I'm sure we are familiar with the famous experiment of Pavlov's dogs, where it was discovered how easily we can, through a psychological process, induce a required behaviour. In the case of Ivan Pavlov, he was ultimately able to produce behaviour of salivation in the dogs when they heard a bell ringing.

This they termed *classical conditioning* and it can be found in any fundamental psychology text book.

The other way of affecting human behaviour is termed *operant conditioning* and basically operates on the basis of rewards and punishments. It is said that our behaviour and motivation is governed by the twin forces of pleasure and pain. As you think about it, our lives are pretty much based upon this concept and it is ubiquitous in society today.

Don't park your car there or you'll get a ticket - (punishment)

Work all month in your job **and get paid** – (reward)

Think about how the concept of reward and punishments (operant conditioning) controls your behaviour. Are you happy about the balance between the level of rewards and punishments in your life?

There may be a correlation (relationship) between the happiness or value in your life and what you do to gain rewards. You may want to consider introducing something in to your lifestyle that brings joy and happiness such as a new hobby or new job.

Someone said to me recently that the message I'm promoting, *"Is not rocket science, it's common sense"*

My response was that I agreed, but what is common sense is definitely not common practice in my research. And incidentally, I highlighted to this individual, if it wasn't rocket science why did they spend 90% of their time complaining about how poor their quality of life was?

Pavlov demonstrated that it was very easy to take someone, in this case a dog, from a bell having no effect at all (unconditioned response) to a point when the bell acted as the trigger for the behaviour (conditioned response) in a short space of time.

In my experience, I would suggest that the phobic person is not really afraid of a spider or of standing on top of a tall building. Instead, the mind has indirectly taught itself to react in a certain way when confronted with the trigger whilst the individual has been in a specific emotion such as anxiety. This is exactly the same psychological process as the Pavlov process.

I have worked with clients who have lived for decades with a debilitating phobia affecting their lives greatly. With every onset of the phobia it reinforces the belief.

A simple way of remembering what fear is:

F – false E – evidence A – appearing R -real

When I work with people on a clinical basis, the first thing I listen to is the way they speak which gives me a direct insight in to their mind.

"We cannot not communicate"

When I talk to people, they 'leak' information which means that, if you know what to look for and how to interpret the signs and signals, you can gain a pretty good insight in to what the person is experiencing.

The way we behave is directly linked to what we believe about a certain thing. The mind will always produce the evidence to support the belief and ultimately the behaviour.

Chapter 9

There is a well known quote by the famous car manufacturer Henry Ford who once said:

"Whether you believe you can or whether you believe you can't, either way you are right".

This expression speaks volumes and gives a clear indication in to the mindset of one of the world's most successful businessmen. Ford understood the power of belief directly affecting behaviour. If you don't believe something is achievable then your behaviour will reflect that and the unconscious mind will see only the 'evidence' to support that belief.

Here are two juxtaposed belief systems that Henry Ford could have subscribed to with regards to his business model which could have been the difference between success and not:

"Nobody will buy cars from me because the car industry is already established, what I am doing is totally new and has never been seen before. It is going to be really difficult for me to change people's thinking"

Or

"My idea is fantastic, never before has my way of doing things been seen. I am going to revolutionise the car industry and as a result I am going, the average family are going to be able own their own car, it will no longer be affordable only to the very affluent".

Which belief do you think Ford subscribed to?

You see, as humans, your behaviour and responses to situations are free flowing from your current belief. The unconscious mind will always produce the evidence to support your belief. When you respond in a certain way to a given situation, your behaviours are linked to a belief about that thing.

A belief is a like a chair, in order for it to stand it needs legs. In our case, the legs are represented by the evidence we see to support our belief. The more 'evidence' we see, the more the belief is reinforced which in turn reinforces the behaviour.

Our beliefs are shaped and influenced by several factors:

Language

Perception

Values

Beliefs

- Language

- Perception

- Values.

- Evidence

When a fishing boat casts out to sea, it uses fishing nets whose size and construction are appropriate for the kinds of fish it intends to catch.

When the fishermen haul in their catch with the nets full of the fish they intended to catch, they obtain evidence that they are using the right tools for the job. So they know by replicating the procedure they will probably yield the same result.

Humans are much the same, when we go in to a situation, say a job interview or other situation; we have a belief or preconceived idea about how the situation will play out. How many times have you wanted to ask for a raise at work or some other awkward situation, do you play through in your mind how you want the meeting to go?

If you think back to the last time you went for a job interview, how were you feeling? What did you say to yourself?

In my experience, most people focus on how they don't want it to go even though they want the job.

"I don't like this; I *always feel nervous and go to pieces when I go for a new job"*

Or

"I'm fed up working for other people, I would like to work for myself and be my own boss but there's no point trying to start a business, it will never work I'm a failure".

When someone makes such statements, it has a very dramatic effect on the unconscious, neurology, the mind and massively affects their experience and perception of a situation. When the person is placed in to the environment such as an interview, or any other situation, all of their preconceived ideas and beliefs come in to play whether they are good or not so good. When the time arrives to cast their psychological fishing net out in to the world, the odds are stacked very much against them if they have been telling their mind over and over how terrible they are in these situations.

Your success and failure really does come down to your feelings and self limiting statement. Just like the fishermen, the fishing net is obedient, it will catch the 'fish' you have asked for. In this case, evidence that you are terrible in these situations.

Now I know that you may be thinking, WHAT! I didn't go in there with the intention of failing. But I'm here to be a little bit in your face and say, "YES YOU DID!"

Every time you thought about interviews and felt bad, every time you told friends you have an interview and told them you hate interviews, every time you played a movie in your head and it went badly, you doomed yourself to failure.

The common response here is, "Yes, but Darren, I don't know any other way, and I don't know all this psychology stuff."

All you need to know here is how the unconscious mind works and how to begin to run your brain even more effectively. Once you grasp this concept that your mind gives you what you ask for, you hold the power in your hand to create massive change.

Let me start by saying this:

I don't want you under any circumstances to:

Picture a big black dog wearing sunglasses driving a red car with black spots on it.

Remember earlier in the book I spoke to you about the Reticular Activating System, the cluster of brain cells affecting processing? The RAS is massively affected by language. When we continually use negative language on ourselves described about, this shapes and adapts the filters in the RAS to either allow or deny pieces of data in to the conscious mind. If we consistently use self limiting language, then the RAS begins to let more and more negative information through and the balance tips from being positive to negative. Even though there are very positive things happening around you, they still remain at the unconscious level. Even though you don't want to feel negative, the RAS believes it is remaining congruent or consistent with what you are asking for.

This relates to the earlier example of where you see people driving the car you want, and wearing the clothes you just bought.

Energy goes where attention flows.

My guess is that you pictured the dog, right?

I would like you to begin to imagine that the RAS is a big control panel with lots of buttons, switches and TV screens. Sat at the controls like a film director is you or someone else of your choosing, real or imagined.

You see it is those buttons, switches and sliders on that control panel that are responsible for your successes and control your behaviour. The panel processes information in a certain way. It will take part of the sentence as a direct command and disregard the rest when we say things to ourselves like:

"I don't want to *feel nervous*"

"I don't want to *fail*"

"The more I feel like walking out of this job *the more stuck I seem to be*"

"I must not *forget to email them today*"

Imagine the captain of a large ocean-going liner stood on the bridge giving orders to the crew in the engine room who pull switches and press buttons in direct response to their orders which in turn controls the direction of the ship. The crew is always obedient and conform to every order without question.

Now imagine yourself as the captain on the bridge, only it is not an ocean-going liner you are controlling and navigating, it is your life, your success, your happiness, your joy, your pain, your failure, your wealth.

This is how the Reticular Activating System affects your wellbeing. When you use the kind of self limiting, negative language such as:

"I can't" "It won't work" "Feel nervous" "Feel anxious" "I never get good luck" "I'm stuck"

what you are doing is instructing the engine room to push buttons, flick switches and take all action necessary in your head to produce the above feelings, thoughts and responses and allow only data that supports that feeling to get through.

Every time you say, think and feel:

I CAN'T, I WON'T, I FEEL ANXIOUS, I FEEL NERVOUS, IT WILL NEVER WORK. I'M NOT, I CAN'T, I WON'T, I NEVER GET GOOD LUCK

every negative statement is a creation and direct command for more and more of the same to the unconscious mind.

By focusing on what you really mean, and phrasing it in the positive, ensures that that you will be sending your metaphorical ship in to very calm, bright, sunny waters and not in to an ice field which may possibly sink the ship. A different set of buttons and switches will be engaged and different more positive 'evidence' will present itself.

The highlighted sections are what hypnosis calls 'embedded commands'. They are unconscious psychological commands or scripts telling the unconscious mind or the engine room what to do. They appear in mail shots, TV advertising, in the most of unlikely of places, anywhere where the intention is to influence and persuade.

Think about the supermarket you go to and the products you buy. Do you think it is a coincidence? It's no coincidence.

Take part in this little experiment.

I want you to look around the room where you are right now and note everything that is red. Everything that is red only.

Then close your eyes and as you do so note everything in the room that is blue.

Don't cheat !!

The chances are, if you followed the instruction, you struggled to see any blue things until you opened your eyes. This is because you told the RAS in your head to filter only for red and by then having to switch to blue confused it.

This is the same in life, actually wanting one thing but through years of emotional scripting and repetition, our unconscious gives us the opposite of what we really want.

We are being psychologically influenced every minute of every day.

Once I realised how this stuff worked, I used to look at junk mail put through the door from credit card companies. What I discovered was that these mailshots were laced with hypnotic language patterns of persuasion and influence.

As a psychological coach and certified clinical hypnotist, I use this technique when I want to introduce a command to the unconscious mind. For example, "As you sit there, reading my book, reading about the mind, *Feeling relaxed*, notice.........as you read, *you are already thinking about your own success and of how you can apply these ideas in your own life.*

It is not difficult, therefore, to understand the concept if you have been brought up, for example, with especially negative or unsupportive parents with self limiting beliefs of their own.

If you were the person who grew up being told by teachers or parents that you would never achieve anything and were told that on a continual basis, then it is not difficult to see how we grow up feeling incomplete and unconfident.

If you have been immersed in this kind of language all your life, you can see that there may be a strong relationship or correlation between the level of success in your life and your current belief systems.

Remember, behaviour is directly linked to belief. A person will always behave in a way that is consistent with their belief.

The good news is, *you can change easily and effortlessly whenever you want to!*

If you have an important job interview, presentation, meeting a prospective partner on a date, meeting new people, a new situation, or even if you just want to improve your general level of confidence, this will work for you.

The word 'but...'is a fantastic example of how language affects perception of something. A classic example could be in a work relationship where someone wants to offer some feedback or criticism.
They may say:

"I think you're doing a fantastic job and the report you did really went down well, *but* you need to focus on the way it was presented in the meeting."

Consider, if this was said to you, where is your focus? On the first part of the statement where you were told about what a fantastic job you are doing or is your focus on the last part of the comment with regards to your presentation style?

I'm guessing you're not giving any attention to the first part but lots to the second, am I right?

Successful people have learnt to replace the word 'but' with 'and', and by doing so changing the whole meaning of what has been said or written.

Let's look at the comment again.

"I think you're doing a fantastic job and the report you did really went down well, ***and*** I'd like you to focus on the way it was presented in the meeting."

There is obviously still the meaning about the concern over the presentation style. However, the unconscious mind of the receiver processes the whole statement rather than just the first part thus avoiding the apparent criticism.

I want you to be begin to notice your own use of the word 'BUT'. Any positive statement you say to yourself, such as, **"I will be confident"**, will be cancelled out if you follow it with the word, 'BUT'. Anything you say prior to the word, no matter how positive it is.

Begin to listen to the way in which you communicate with yourself.
There are certain words in the English language that have a very profound impact on the human mind. Listen to the following expressions and note if you use any of them yourself.

I must....... I should be........ I've got to....... I ought to....... I don't have a choice...... I'll try..........

'I'll try' is a great statement for demonstrating and producing absolutely no intention, commitment or motivation at all. The words 'try' has a very definite meaning in the English language. If I said, "I tried to open the door," it means I was not successful.

When we use the word 'try' it gives the unconscious a clear instruction. It is a presupposition or assertion that failure will follow.

When we speak to someone, the words we use play a massive part in how that person is processing the information. If we asked someone to do a task for us that they knew was important to us but replied with, "I'll try and do it," how motivated and committed to completing the task are they?

Not much is my guess.

Sound familiar? Those expressions are very disempowering. They have a distinct effect on the unconscious mind. They tell you that you do not have choice and control.

Beginning to replace these words with some of the following will produce much more powerful momentum for you.

I will..... I am..... I am willing to..... I plan to .... Yes........

For example, "As you sit there, reading my book, reading about the mind, *feeling relaxed*, notice.........as you read, *you are already thinking about how you are going to apply these ideas in your life."*

The good news is, *you can change easily and effortlessly whenever you want to!*

If you have an important job interview, or presentation, meeting a prospective partner on a date, meeting new people, a new situation, or even if you just want to improve your general level of confidence, this will work for you.

Are you frustrated or unhappy with your life or some other issue where your current belief or way of thinking is shifting your energy and focus in one area preventing you from seeing the simple solution?

Task:

I want you to find a place where you can relax and not be bothered by the phone ringing or people bothering you for at least 5 minutes.

I want you to think about a situation that is coming up or could come up where you would like greater confidence or some other positive personal quality.

Close your eyes and notice what you say to yourself and write it down, notice how you feel and where you notice these feelings.

If it's a job interview or some other social situation such as a date, begin to run a movie in your head of the perfect outcome. Notice how good it feels.

The first part of change is awareness, if you are not aware of something, then how can you do anything about it?

I want you to then write down what you saw, felt and heard.

If you didn't like what you saw, replay the film and allow your unconscious to play the film but now begin to 'direct' the film in the way you want it.

What positive things can you say to yourself as you run the film?

Whatever you intend to do will be affected where your energy and focus is directed.

"I want to feel confident in my interview."

I will be saying to myself, "I am very good at interviews".

Many people attribute feelings to a colour like red for anger and blue for calmness. Whatever colour you feel is right; imagine you are sitting bathed in this colour as you think about your interview or other situation.

As we shall see later, different ways of thinking about things are immensely powerful and sometimes even life changing and many successful people use psychological techniques to improve their chances of success.

By saying to yourself:

"I am confident, I am prepared. I am very happy and calm when I attend interviews,"

you are giving direct commands to your control panel which in turn will begin to activate the appropriate buttons and switches just like the captain of a ship giving orders to the crew.

It may well not feel real or may feel like a kind of a lie at first, but if you work with the process, like I mentioned earlier, science tells us that if you do something for a period of 21 days then it becomes a habitual behaviour.

Remember:

  • Your experience will always remain consistent with your belief about something.

  • Your mind will always seek out the 'evidence' to support the belief.

The challenge that I notice with people is that, although they know that they want something different, they focus on what they don't want and not want they do want.

When I spoke to clients in my practice, I always used to begin the session by asking clients the magic question:

"What is it that you want?"

Nine times out of ten clients would then reply:

"Well, *I don't want to feel like this and I don't want to always do that* ..."

It is very important that when you are making changes in your life, you begin by stating your goal, or what I shall call 'outcome', in a positive tense.

To illustrate, let's say you don't have much money in your bank account at the moment and times are hard. Although times are hard, I want you to listen to what you say to yourself or the way you are thinking and feeling when you think about your finances.

Most people focus on the scarcity or lack of money, or the debt they are in. Now, I know you may be sitting there thinking, What, just by thinking about money differently is going to bring me more in?

Well actually, YES!

Believe me, I do understand how the scarcity of money can affect you, even destroy you, especially in today's financial climate.

Scientists have discovered that on average we have at least 60,000 separate thoughts each day. Now obviously we couldn't consciously process that kind of workload. Your thoughts act as a feedback mechanism, just like the rocket to the Moon we spoke about earlier, that lets you understand whether you're on track with what it is you want.

When you are feeling low or not as you would like, learn to ask yourself the question, "What am I focusing on at the moment?" The chances are that you are focusing on the negatives.

Most people think that we attract thoughts by default, that is that we have no conscious control over our thoughts. Your thoughts cause your feelings, one makes you feel good and the other makes you feel bad.
This in turn affects the way in which you respond to situations.

Rather than focusing on money from the viewpoint of:

"I don't earn enough money, I am tired and bored of having no money and always having to go without."

If someone wanted a strategy to feel bad, I am sure you'll agree this is a brilliant one to implement. I would challenge anyone to say the statement above each day every day for 21 days and not feel bad when they think about their finances.

Although you may not have enough money, the secret is not to focus on scarcity and lack of money because that places all of your focus and energy on what you don't want. Your psychological fishing net will give you even more of how bad it is.

I want your mind *to **let you know every time your focus shifts to the negative.***

Get in to the habit of saying something like:

"Money comes to me easily and effortlessly"

Or

"I am already starting to have ideas that will attract even more money".

It sounds very simple but, believe me, when if you do this for a minimum of 21 days, you will begin to notice opportunities around you that you never before thought possible. Focus on the end result and notice the positive feelings that are produced.

Why am I so sure this stuff works?

The book you have in your hand is the physical manifestation of visual motor rehearsal. I imagined very vividly what my book would look like, what it would feel like for my book to be in bookstores and for me to be meeting people at book signings. How I would feel to receive emails telling me how my ideas have helped people.

It has all come true, just like I imagined it.

I know this sounds crazy but even if you think it's crazy just do it. If it's worked for me, it will work for you. Even if you can't see the opportunities at the moment, they really are there. Have faith and trust me.

One principle I believe in with all of my being is:

If it's possible for one person, then it's possible for you and me.

You have the same mental process and physiology as anyone else you have seen achieve phenomenal success. However, in order to change your circumstances, you must first change your thinking and have faith in yourself and the process.

"You don't need to see the whole staircase in order to take the first step in faith, just take the first step."

Martin Luther King

Start today by saying to yourself something like:

"I am so happy that *I have started to make changes* and I already know that *my situation is not permanent*, I will *begin now to attract even more money* to me so that *I can have a better life, the process had already begun the moment I chose this book"*

Can you see how the highlighted embedded commands are much more empowering which in turn will direct your thoughts, feelings and beliefs about money?

Whatever you think about, you bring about.

What you visualise, you materialise.

Remember, wherever you are in your life right now is only your current reality. Your current position is a result of thoughts and feelings you thought yesterday, last week, last month etc. Today is a brand new day. It is never too late to make changes.

People look at their current situation and say, *"This is who I am!"*
They define themselves by their current situation. This is not who you are, this is who you were before you began making a decision to make changes and possibly reading this book.

Your current situation is the result of your previous thoughts and actions not the future ones. So we are currently living in the residual of yesterday. When you define yourself by your previous thought, achievement and actions, you doom yourself to failure.

Tomorrow never comes, but today is already here!

Even if you dismiss 99% of everything I have presented in this book so far, even by changing by 1% today, if you continue on that small level, your life will be 365% better by this time next year.

What would that mean to you?

Imagine two ships in harbour preparing to set sail. They are side by side with one slight difference; one of the ships has its course set one degree different to the other.

Now, if you imagine just how small a percentage it is out of 360°, once the ships set sail they remain side by side. However, once they leave the harbour and they continue to move through the water out to sea, it is only when the ships have taken sufficient action that the difference begins to get noticeable. Once out to sea, the ship with the 1 degree difference begins to veer off in a different direction very noticeably. And there will come a point when the two ships would lose sight of each other.

This demonstrates how consciously making a minute change in the way we are currently thinking can ultimately place us in a very different place.

When people decide to make changes in their life, they take a little action and when they don't get the results straight away they lose motivation and lose focus and the old habits creep back in, saying these techniques don't work. Just like the ships in port, you need to take the appropriate action and leave the port and get out to sea.

People who seem to have everything, they have already learnt the process they need to do before results come.

The cycle of learning

I used to go to the circus with my parents. Even at a young age, I was amazed at how one person could control and appear to harness the sheer strength and might of the massive elephants at the circus. What prevented them from escaping and running away?

The simple answer is, belief.

Belief is what makes the difference between Mother Teresa and Adolf Hitler.

The belief in where you are right now controls and governs your opportunities for tomorrow, just as the thoughts, feelings and beliefs you thought yesterday govern your reality today.

"All we are is the result of what we have thought"

Buddha

Fig 1.

Fig 2.

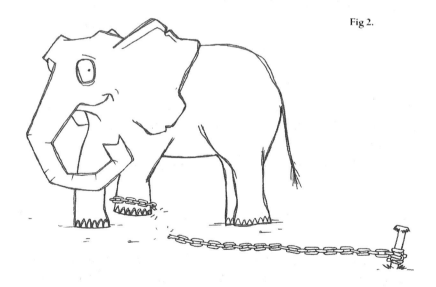

When elephants are very young, they are tethered to the ground with a chain around their foot secured in the ground by a stake. Like most of us who were confined by chains would, they try to escape. They try and try by pulling this way and that on the chains until, like the fleas in the jar, they reach a point of futility where they no longer even try to escape. This is because, as a result of taking repeated action, a new self limiting belief has become wired in to their neurology.

What can we learn from this?

Once they have gained this belief that the more they try to escape and don't, the deeper the belief becomes ingrained in to their mind.

Now the restraints can be removed and the elephant will never again try to escape because the 'evidence' of all the previous attempts to escape come to mind. This is the reason one of Nature's most revered and powerful animals can be controlled by a mere child and the very same reason so many of us in life do not achieve what we want and settle for mediocrity.

When we attempt to do something, we think back to the times we took action and didn't get the result we wanted, the same process as the elephant. The psychological process is exactly the same. The difference we have as humans is that although sometimes it doesn't feel like it, we really do have choice in our life unlike many animals that go with what is happening to them.

In hypnosis, we call this process the **law of reversal effect,** where we have x affecting y, or one *cause (x) affecting (y) another.*

An example of this in a clinical setting can be illustrated when a hypnotherapist treating a client who is showing some resistance to relaxation as part of their hypnotic induction may introduce certain suggestions to the unconscious mind. One such 'suggestion' may be:

"The more your body resists relaxation, the deeper you recognise you are beginning to breath".

One cancels out the other. I have often heard clients say things like:

"The harder I try to work on my new business, the more problems I seem to have"

Or

"Whenever I attend an interview, I always seem to go to pieces."

This is a kind of self hypnosis and if said frequently enough becomes a self limiting belief creating all sorts of confidence issues.

As you sit there reading this book, I want you to cross your arms in the way you have done thousands of times previously.

Next, I want you to unfold them and then cross them in the opposite way.

Can you cross them immediately without thinking or was there a split second when your brain kicked in and had to think about the task?

This is because it is believed that any behaviour done on a continual basis for 21 days or more becomes habitual. The reason your brain had to think about it was that the second time you were asking it to think about something it has not had to consider before.

There is also a psychological principle known as **self-fulfilling prophecy.**

If you grew up with unsupportive parents or maybe you have a negative partner or indeed you feel negative, it has been proven that we become what we think about. So, if you are called stupid enough times then you will unconsciously begin to take on the belief that you are.

As you think about it now, are your current beliefs about where you are in your life, consistent with your current situation? My guess is yes!

New thoughts, feelings and behaviours always feel a little strange and unfamiliar at first but *the more you practise them the easier it becomes.*

Did you notice the deliberate language pattern I slipped in there to influence you?

Chapter 10

In psychology, there is the age old debate called the *nature vs. nurture* debate which when simplified very simply states that we are all genetically programmed to be a certain sort of person which means your outcome is already predetermined and there are things in your nature and physiology that you simply cannot change or nurture, that is, you become a product of your environment, whatever you think about, you bring about.

To date, there has been no finite conclusion as to which theory is correct. However, both are very plausible as there are clearly infinite neurological functions happening in our brains. We all share the same neurophysiology.

For me, I believe that we undoubtedly inherit certain genetic traits from our parents. However, I also believe that whatever you focus on is what you get.

For me history is littered with people who, according to the odds, should have never been successful as we shall discuss later.

If your father achieved only limited success in life, does this mean that you are genetically predetermined to achieve only a similar level of success?

For me, no. I am in the business of creating my own opportunities and successes as I hope you are too.

Scientists discovered many years ago that the mind and the body are linked. That is to say, that whatever we think about affects the physiology, nervous system and brain chemistry. When we think a thought there are literally infinite amounts of changes in the body which for the most part go unnoticed. However, to the trained eye they are immediately observable.

Have you ever seen a member of your family, a co-worker or friend and known instantly by looking at them that something was wrong? Of course, that is because you have learnt that when a certain posture is adopted this displays their true feelings on the inside.

When we think about ideas or memories, they not only affect the way we think and feel but they produce observable physiological and psychological changes. When we take actors, for example, who when playing a particularly emotional scene, are trained to think back to a time in the past from personal experience to access the appropriate feeling or state of mind. This is so they can produce an even better performance.

When we think about feelings and memories, both good and bad, as far as the mind and body are concerned the same parts of the brain will engage and the same neurones and muscles will fire. This is because the mind cannot distinguish between things real or imagined.

These techniques have been used by everyone from NASA to very successful sportspeople, business people and even politicians. The technique is known as VISUAL MOTOR REHEARSAL. or is sometimes called MENTAL REHEARSAL.

When we imagine something, vividly and consistently over and over again, it becomes hardwired in to our nervous system like learning to drive a car. When we go to do the skills for real, the mind does not perceive that we are doing this for the first time. Because we have mentally rehearsed it thousands of times, the mind just sees this as one of those times and you get the result you have only previously imagined.

I use this skill myself when doing public speaking and also when working with clients of how I want things to go.

Many years ago there was a famous experiment to test the theory of mental rehearsal. Two groups of people were gathered together. Group A were to be immersed in the world of skiing for 30 days. None of the group had ever skied previously but they would eat, breathe and sleep the world of skiing for the 30 days.

The second group B would also spend 30 days learning to ski. However, they would never go within 10 feet of a ski slope. During the experiment, Group B were made to watch hundreds of hours of film of athletes skiing. They were then asked to 'associate' or step in to the heads of the athletes, to imagine where the sensations, feelings and tensions would be in their bodies as they negotiated tight bends and jumps. This process was done time after time after time so that the process became hardwired in to their neurology.

The two groups were never allowed to associate until the end of the experiment.

The startling thing was that when Group B was finally taken to a real ski slope, their level of competency far outweighed their counterparts in group A. Group B subjects could not explain how or why it was so but they said they could just ski and felt like it was something they just knew how to do.

The brains of both groups were connected to sophisticated biofeedback machines to measure brain activity during the training phase. The startling thing was that the brain activity of those in Group B matched the brain waves of subjects in Group A, even though they had not yet set foot on the ski slope for real. The same muscles were engaged and the same neurones fired in the brain. Therefore they concluded that the brain cannot differentiate between things that are real or imagined. A person becomes what they think about.

This technique has been mapped out and used by entrepreneurs, athletes, astronauts and many more.

The following is a very powerful mental rehearsal technique designed to move yourself away from the things that no longer serve you and towards the things you desire.

"He who would search for pearls must dive below."

John Dryden

Task

I want you to think about some event that could be happening for you soon, such as an interview or going in to some new situation which under normal circumstances would cause you some concern. The difference is that I want you to imagine you are watching a movie of the event up there on the big screen like in the cinema. See yourself in full colour in that environment. If you don't have an event looming in your life just imagine where you want changes in your life. Is it a new car, new house, relationship, confidence, assertiveness, whatever it is, you have the resources within you or you can recreate them. Imagine you are a movie director in which you are the star. See yourself up there on the screen as if you were looking at another you.

What does the you up on the screen need to do in order to demonstrate being excellent?

How is the you up there on the screen standing?

How does the you up there on the screen feel?

What are your posture and facial expression like?

Notice the positive things. The you up there on the screen says to themselves:

"I can do it" "I will be my best" "Nothing can stop me!" "I always get good luck" "Success comes to me easily and effortlessly"

Now you may have a favourite piece of music or another favourite sound. Hear it now in full surround sound in your mind as you continue to see the images and hear the sounds around you. Close your eyes and really zoom in on the experience, see what you see, hear what you hear and notice the feelings.

If you could give the you up there a colour that encompassed their experience, what would it be? Red or orange, purple or blue or something else?

Now when you have created the perfect scene in your mind, I want you in your imagination to walk towards the screen where the other you is located and after taking a very deep breath, I want you to step in to the screen and step in to the other you. Begin to feel the power and energy that begins to flow through you as you become the other you.

See the place through the new perspective that was until now only up on the screen.

Breathe deeply, that's right. Continue to see, hear and feel how good it feels to be in this new frame of mind with all of the positive language you have chosen to use now.

When you are feeling this good, what new belief does the new you need to believe in order to keep these positive feelings?

Allow the film to play out, and this can be as long or as short as you like. The importance lies in the positive feelings this experience gives you.

Notice how changing the colour and sounds in the picture affects the power and emotive feelings you experience.

Now I know at this point you may be thinking, What am I doing Darren? This all seems a bit strange,

That's good. Remember, the mind once stretched by new ideas, never regains its original dimension.

I would like you to invest 10 minutes every day visualising yourself being fantastic in your movie. Follow the procedure of stepping in to the you on the screen. You can use this very powerful visual motor rehearsal technique for any future event.

Now, if you have followed my instructions, think about the future event you chose for your film when you used to feel unconfident or unsure. As you think about it now, do you notice the changes in how you feel towards it?

You may need to change certain aspects of the film to make it an even better experience.

Some people say, "Really, do I need to do this every day?"

Yes, how badly do you want change?

In a day that's made up of 1,440 minutes, I'm asking you to invest just 10 of them in yourself.

Any behaviour we have has been a result of repetition. The most simple way of changing old habits and acquiring new positive empowering behaviours is to be aware of their triggers and of when we are unconsciously slipping in to the old unwanted habits. Set the intention every day for your mind to give you a signal that you will know when you are slipping.

The first step to becoming excellent and making rapid and effective changes is called:

'interrupting the pattern'

Imagine now that you are meeting someone for the first time, maybe at work or some other formal occasion. You reach out your hand to shake hands with someone and they extend their hand towards you. However, just before you touch hands, they suddenly pull their hand away from you and put it to their face and make a funny gesture which surprises you. This would be an example of a pattern interrupt. It is the confusion that follows when something does not follow its usual path such as a handshake. There is a definite beginning, middle and an end in the cycle of a handshake and when this cycle is not completed it throws the unconscious mind in to a state of confusion.

If you were suddenly plunged in to a faraway land with a very different culture, it would feel very strange. If, in the new land, this was their way of shaking hands you would soon adopt this unusual custom. If your unconscious did the action enough times it would soon forget the way in which you used to shake hands.

If you are going to be in a situation you are not confident in, notice your body's response in line with the old behaviour.

Make the conscious effort to immediately run your film in your head where you are excellent. This will have the same effect on the unconscious mind as with the handshake.

When we used to think about say, giving a presentation and we used to say things to ourselves and notice that terrible feeling of dread, when we begin to run the film of being very good at giving presentations with the positive feelings, it interrupts the old pattern and begins to use the new one. Very soon, the evidence the self limiting belief used to use to support itself is no longer present and new evidence is discovered to support the new positive belief. This confuses the old self limiting belief and behaviour like the handshake and by quickly thinking about the new behaviour, you will notice very, very quickly, your response will change in line with the new belief.

Remember!

Anything we do as humans for a period of 21 days or more begins to become an habitual behaviour.

A few inspirational stories

There was a famous story surrounding the famous American basketball player, Magic Johnson. He was to be paid many millions of dollars to appear in a *Pepsi Cola* advertisement. The commercial surrounded Magic Johnson shooting the ball at the basket and missing.

As his abilities were built on the foundation of thousands and thousands of hours of practice, the process of scoring a point by dunking the ball in the basket had become hardwired in to his neurology which allowed him to have a very high success rate.

The film crew attempted in excess of 300 takes to capture Magic missing the basket. The act of consciously missing the basket went against his belief system, and the skills that had been hardwired in to his neurology prevented him from producing a result that was not consistent with his belief.

Roger Bannister

Back in the 1950s there was a young athlete by the name of Roger Bannister. You may have heard of him or maybe you haven't. However, he holds a place in the history books for his ground breaking achievement of running a mile in under four minutes on the 6th of May 1954. Until that time, no one had ever completed such an achievement. Following the event, Bannister is quoted as saying:

"No longer conscious of my movement, I discovered a new unity with nature. I had found a new source of power and beauty, a source of power I had never dreamt existed."

Again, this demonstrates a clear of thinking in to one of history's most famous athletes.

What Bannister did was take the lid off the jam jar in athletics, in respect of the way others later saw the breaking of the four-minute mile. The psychological glass ceiling was shattered because they were shown evidence that contradicted the current way they saw the four-minute mile. Until that day everyone believed it was physically impossible, but following his achievement, other athletes achieved even better times than Roger.

Did you ever hear of a man named Cliff Young? Many people haven't.

In 1981, the then 61-year-old sheep and potato farmer in Australia had one dream, to compete in the Westfield Sydney to Melbourne ultra marathon which took place over many days and was a distance of 544 miles. He had no formal training, no specialist equipment or special diet and no preconceived ideas. In preparation he had been running after his sheep in his field three times a day.

His only outcome was to run and take part. But what was interesting was that what he achieved changed for ever the way in which athletes would run.

Whilst competing in the five, people laughed at the way he ran as he shuffled along in his big boots and overalls.

Due to the distance, the rules of the race allowed athletes a short period of sleep to rest. However, Cliff denied himself sleep and even when his competitors were sleeping he just kept going. And what was amazing was that Cliff not only won the race but beat the previous record by 2 days.

When he was interviewed by the media he said, "*I just imagined that I was chasing my sheep in the field and there was a bad storm coming in from behind me.*"

He became the epitome of the tortoise and hare fable. He became a national hero in Australia and an inspirational figure for thousands of people. When he died in 2003 over a thousand people attended his funeral.

Another story that I want to tell you concerns a man called Harland Sanders. He may not sound too familiar but you may know him better as Colonel Sanders who founded the famous *Kentucky Fried Chicken* chain.

Now, although *KFC* can be seen in pretty much any town throughout the entire world, did you ever consider where it all began?

He was born in Indiana in the United States in 1890 and during his very varied life, he had many jobs. By the age of 40 he was running a service station in Kentucky and serving chicken out of a window of the family's house because the gas station did not have a restaurant. But the popularity of his unique style of cooking chicken grew and grew.

Some years later he eventually moved in to a 142-seat restaurant where he spent a good few years perfecting his recipe and building up the business and word quickly spread about the fantastic tasting chicken. The business went from strength to strength and people flocked to the restaurant to taste this strange-looking man's chicken recipe. However, many years later, disaster struck when a new interstate was due to be constructed near to the restaurant. Once completed, Harland saw his business begin to suffer and the customers grew less and less as the route of the new interstate diverted much or all of his passing trade. And the steady decline in customers eventually forced him in to a situation where he had no choice but admit defeat and close the restaurant.

Now at the age of 65, having lost everything he had built up over the past 25 years, he withdrew $105 from his first social security cheque from the government. This he used to begin to visit different restaurants trying to get them to sign up as a franchisee, in the hope he could rebuild what he once had. He asked restaurant owners to use his 'secret recipe of herbs and spices' and put it on their menus in exchange for a few cents for every sale.

"For they conquer who believe they can."
<u>John Dryden</u>

It is reported that Colonel Sanders received in excess of 2,000 rejections from different restaurants in response to his business preposition, being eventually saved by the owner of the America burger chain, *Wendy's*. The owner eventually agreed to help him and the rest, as they say, is history.

In 1964, at the age of 74, Harland Sanders sold the entire company to a group of entrepreneurs for a reported $2 million. Although he had sold the company, he was still a shareholder and the new owner retained his services as the face of the *Kentucky Fried Chicken* brand. He spent the rest of his life going around every *KFC* in America doing personal appearances in his trademark white suit and white beard. He died in 1980 at the age of 90.

His achievement continues today with the Sanders Trust which donates millions of dollars to charities each year.

What would have been if he had not had the passion, belief and motivation to achieve his goals? If we were to break down the psychology of the story, you can see that he followed the same basic process as I have already presented:

1. Knowing your outcome.

2. Taking massive action.

3. Responding to feedback.

4. Being flexible.

What can we learn from this?

In order for these individuals to have achieved what they achieved, they all had to have a 100% unwavering belief in what they were doing and the passion to continue to take action and learn from their results.

Be honest with yourself, how many restaurant rejections would it have taken in order for you to have given up - 1, 12, 50, 1,000? How many people would keep going once they had had over 2,000 rejections?

I am not saying that you need to experience that amount of rejection. However, by following the same blueprint in your life, you will be following the masters in history. You can achieve success in whatever you want. Not everyone wants to be a Cliff Young, a Roger Bannister or indeed a Colonel Sanders. But if you begin today to consciously divert your focus away from the things in your life right now that don't serve you and cause you pain and unhappiness and instead begin to direct them towards things that you want, such as more wealth, health, happiness, love, joy even if it is not there at the moment. As far as the brain is concerned you will have already achieved these goals and this in turn will affect your belief system and become wired in to your neurology. Your belief and desire in what you want will expand and get stronger and the old unwanted areas in your life will fall away and disappear.

"Energy goes where your attention flows"

Begin to imagine that your focus and attention are like a finely tuned laser beam. You will illuminate whatever and wherever you point it.

Begin to consciously make pictures in your head and write down positive statements and run those in your mind in relation to where you want to go. You wouldn't get in to your car without having a destination in mind would you? The mind is exactly the same; it will take you in whatever direction you point it.

A fantastic technique for snapping yourself out of a less than productive state of mind is to first change your physiology. If you are sitting down, get up and literally move your arms and legs around. If you have ever attended one of my lectures or seminars, you will know that the audience are regularly asked to move quickly around the room. This energizers the body very quickly. There is a connection between mind and body and physiology plays a massive part in your thoughts and feelings.

Next think about a great time from the past, your wedding, the birth of a child, buying your first house, graduating from college, passing your driving test. If you can't think of a great memory make one up, imagine what you would do if you won the lottery, met the Queen, I don't care. Close your eyes and begin to notice the positive feelings that are free flowing from your thoughts. You may have a favourite piece of music that you like driving to or running to that gets you 'in the zone'. Remember, the mind cannot differentiate between things real or imagined.

During the course of the book, I have sought to give you an understanding of the power of our minds.

As things come up in your life now, what will be different from this moment on?

Rather than run the same old patterns of behaviour, notice how you are thinking and what you currently believe about the situation. Is your current way of thinking what you want?

Practise setting small outcomes, that way you will need to take only a small amount of action in order to achieve your goal and this will seek to reinforce a new belief from the start.

Write down your daily successes and review them weekly.

I am very excited for you as you begin your journey and begin jumping out of your jar.

A final word and a poem to see you on your way as we near the end of our time together. During the course of the book, I have aimed to raise your awareness of your own situation and of how you really can begin to change things in your life right now. The stark reality though is that I can't be with you 24 / 7. The change must come from within you. You are the one who must now accept personal responsibility for where you are and ultimately where you are going. The thoughts and feelings that are coursing through your mind and body right now influence the direction in which you will steer your life from this moment on.

You will either wake up tomorrow in your old life, running the same patterns of behaviour you have run all of your life. These being the same old beliefs about life which have always given you the same old results.

Though the alternative perhaps may be that tonight while you sleep and dream and dream and sleep, all of the learning you have made during the course of reading this book *will have percolated through your mind and taken root* so when you wake tomorrow, you may be surprised, *delightfully*, at how different you may indeed feel towards the exciting journey that awaits you.

You now get it that you are the architect of your own life. The rest of the story is up to you. The outcome is whatever you say it is.

And now a poem that has both inspired and motivated me through some very dark times. I now give it to you in the hope it will help you in times of when you need inspiration.

DON'T QUIT

When things go wrong, as they sometimes will,
When the road you're trudging seems all uphill,
When the funds are low and the debts are high,
And you want to smile, but you have to sigh,
When care is pressing you down a bit,
Rest, if you must, but don't you quit.

Life is strange with its twists and turns,
As every one of us sometimes learns,
And many a failure turns about,
When he might have won had he stuck it out;
Don't give up though the pace seems slow--
You may succeed with another blow.

Often the goal is nearer than,
It seems to a faint and faltering man,
Often the struggler has given up,
When he might have captured the victor's cup,
And he learned too late when the night slipped down,
How close he was to the golden crown.

Success is failure turned inside out--
The silver tint of the clouds of doubt,
And you never can tell how close you are,
It may be near when it seems so far,
So stick to the fight when you're hardest hit--
It's when things seem worst that you must not quit.

- Author unknown

I want you to jump, jump and jump again. Never stop jumping until you finally achieve everything you want in your life, until you leave the confines of your jam jar.

Until we meet again, keep the faith.

Darren

Let me know your JAM JAR successes.

Email me at : info@darrenstanton.com